ENGLISH COSTUME IN
THE AGE OF ELIZABETH

Other books in this series

ENGLISH COSTUME
OF THE EARLY MIDDLE AGES
THE 10th TO THE 13th CENTURIES
by IRIS BROOKE

ENGLISH COSTUME
OF THE LATER MIDDLE AGES
THE 14th AND 15th CENTURIES

ENGLISH COSTUME
OF THE SEVENTEENTH CENTURY
by IRIS BROOKE

ENGLISH COSTUME
OF THE EIGHTEENTH CENTURY
by IRIS BROOKE and JAMES LAVER

ENGLISH COSTUME
OF THE NINETEENTH CENTURY
by IRIS BROOKE and JAMES LAVER

ENGLISH CHILDREN'S COSTUME
SINCE 1775   by IRIS BROOKE
Introduction by JAMES LAVER

1520

English Costume

in the

Age of Elizabeth

The Sixteenth Century

Drawn and Described by
IRIS BROOKE

Adam & Charles Black

First Published 1933
Reprinted 1938
Second Edition 1950
Reprinted 1956, 1967, 1972, 1973, 1977
A & C Black Ltd
35 Bedford Row, London wc1r 4jh
© A & C Black Ltd
isbn 0 7136 0156 6

Reproduced by Colourcraftsmen Ltd
Printed in Great Britain by Tindal Press
Chelmsford, Essex

FOREWORD

ALTHOUGH this book bears the title "The Age of Elizabeth," it actually covers the entire sixteenth century. To show the evolution and slow, steady development of costume it is necessary to go back to structural beginnings : the trunk-hose, the flat wool caps, and numerous other equally interesting details of dress in Elizabethan England—all had their origin in the Courts of Henry VII and Henry VIII.

Elizabeth's reign was a magnificent pageantry of exotic and fantastic costume, unrivalled in our history, which had its inspiration in the glamour of her father's Court, and owed its ultimate execution to the influx of riches into a country impoverished by recent royal extravagances. There was a notable increase in the refinements of domestic life, and with the coming of panelled rooms, latticed windows, and carpeted floors, an altogether higher degree of personal fastidiousness was displayed. Not only was more attention paid to dress, but cosmetics were introduced from the Indies, and so were several new and exciting perfumes ; both these innovations tended to give a more cultivated finish to an exotic costume.

Competition, always an important factor in the history of costume, became a potent impulse, capable of greater gratification then ever before in this age when Englishmen were first journeying beyond the sea in search of commerce or adventure. A new skirt from Spain, a new hat from Italy, a hat-band from France, a slashed bombasted doublet from Germany—all were possessions to be coveted. And so it was throughout the century, each man vying with his neighbour for the possession of the greatest number and variety of enviable articles of adornment.

It is clearly impossible to illustrate here more than a small fraction of the designs that may be found in contemporary manuscripts, wall-paintings, portraits, miniatures, effigies, and actual garments still surviving. Equally impracticable would be any complete description of the minute and myriad methods of ornamentation which, in this period of most complex costume, adorned practically every item of apparel from hat to shoes. I have aimed, therefore, to condense and simplify, so that in these few hundred drawings may be found representative and typical examples of the garments which in all probability were the daily wear of our predecessors some four centuries ago.

I. B.

ENGLISH COSTUME
IN THE AGE OF ELIZABETH

1500—1510

WHEN the sixteenth century opened, the wealthy were spending vast sums on clothes. At the wedding of Prince Arthur and Catharine of Aragon in 1501 the Duke of Buckingham wore " a gowne wrought of needle worke and set upon cloth of tissue, furr'd with sables, the which gowne was valued at £1500. Sir Nicholas Vause, knight, wore a gowne of purple velvet dight with pieces of gold, so thick and massie that it was valued in golde besides the silke and fur a thousand pounde. Very wonderful it was to behold the riches of apparel worn that day, with puissant chaines of gold, of which two were specially noted, to wit : Sir T. Brandon, knight, master of the king's horse, which wore a chain valued at 1400 pound, and the other, W. de Rivers, esquire, master of the kinges haukes, which chain was valued at a thousand pound." And it should be realized that money then possessed many times its value to-day.

Men's clothes were not only costly but so rich in their variety that it is now barely possible to distinguish all their pieces as individual garments. So numerous were the additions of sleeves, skirts, fronts, and other spare parts that we cannot state definitely of what the complete costume consisted. The body-garment, however, may be assumed to have been five separate pieces. First, the shirt ; here at least we are safe, for the shirt was the foundation garment and always had sleeves. It was made of holland, cambric, or lawn, and frequently it was embroidered. The neck-line was low and showed the collar-bone, occasionally so low that it scarcely covered the shoulders ; more often it was round than square in cut. The sleeves were full and loose to the wrist, where they were finished with a tiny band or frill.

Over the shirt was worn the doublet, which may or may not have had sleeves. Sometimes, too, the sleeves were separate pieces tied at the shoulders with points, and showed the shirt underneath through the gaps. The doublet was usually padded and rarely reached below the waist during the first ten years of the century. Next came the jerkin or coat, similar in cut to the doublet, though it usually had sleeves of some sort, either long or to the elbow. Sometimes it was skirted, or the skirts might be entirely separate affairs, it which case they were termed *basses*.

1500—1510 (*continued*)

A gown, or more rarely a cloak, was worn over the jerkin. Usually made of some heavy woollen material and lined with fur, this could touch the ground or barely reach to the knee, as pleased its owner. Finally, men wore from the waist to the foot an entire garment—tights, hose, or stocks. These, as you may see, were simple and tight-fitting at the beginning of the century. A tendency to adorn the upper part with slashing and embroidery was the first sign of the eventual trunk-hose, predominant throughout the period. By about 1510 upper-stocks had definitely assumed the aspect of separate breeches, although actually this was not the case. These were made of cloth or velvet, cut on the cross of the material to give the necessary elasticity and stretch; knitted hose were not introduced till much later in the century.

Shoes were flat-soled, like a mule without a heel, though occasionally an inch or so of leather was added as a covering for the heel. Boots of soft coloured leather were worn for riding.

Occasionally we see examples of "rush" shoes, made of plaited straw or reeds, and worn by the peasantry. These were worn over the entire foot, and the loose ends of rush formed a rough fringe around the ankle. This type of footgear seems to have been worn extensively on the Continent, and the paintings of Hans Holbein the elder show us numerous varieties. Clogs also were not unknown on this side of the Channel.

1500—1510 (*continued*)

Women's dress, although by our modern standards distinctly complicated, was actually exceedingly simple, except in rare cases when the slashing actually cut the gown into separate parts.

First was worn the shift, similar in cut to the man's shirt; then one or two petticoats, the upper one often pleated and of a contrasting colour to the gown; then the gown itself, with full trailing skirts. In some instances the train was lifted and fastened to the girdle at the back, to show the lining, and to facilitate walking. The gown was either laced at the back or fastened in front. The neck was square and low in front, and V or U shaped at the back. Its sleeves were usually bell-shaped, with the lower edge turned back several inches to form immense cuffs which revealed the lining and displayed the sleeves underneath, which were attached to the elbow or shoulder. Plain, full sleeves, tight at the wrist, were still very popular, and there are numerous examples of tied and slashed sleeves. Also the entirely separate sleeve, tied in four or five points at the shoulder and showing the puffed shift through the gaps, was frequently worn.

Belts and girdles were a necessary part of dress for both sexes. The men had a pouch or purse hung from one side with a slit behind to hold the dagger; this fashion, however, was superseded almost at the beginning of the century by a separate sheath and dagger attached to the right-hand side of the belt. The woman's girdle was made of cord or chain, and from it hung a miscellaneous collection of household requisites, anything, in fact, from keys to a book.

Clothes were slashed, embroidered, furred, and guarded— that is, having wide bands of velvet (usually black) or embroidery sewn on the garment as a form of decoration. Precious stones, gold and silver chains and clasps, and numerous rings were worn extensively. Gloves, when worn, were cut at the knuckles to show the rings beneath.

1 5 0 0—1 5 1 0 (*continued*)

Male headgear might be described under two categories :
the *biretta*, and the beret, very similar to that worn to-day
but with a brim, usually turned up and cut in one or more
places to make flaps, which frequently overlapped. Women's
head-dress was less simple. The Dutch *coif*, or cap, was
worn quite frequently in England. This consisted of one
tight-fitting cap over the front of the head, with the hair
piled up in a great coil behind it, and over this the actual
coif, usually made of embroidered lawn. Young unmarried
girls frequently wore their hair loose, or tied with a " snood,"
or tucked into a gold net after the French style. While the
definite English tendency was for the *coif* and veil, its popularity was challenged about 1503 by the gable head-dress,
which lasted with modifications for forty years or more.
The gable head-dress was the roof-like arrangement worn
by the second figure on the preceding page. This particular
example shows the earliest type with the long side-pieces,
which later were folded back across the top of the " gable."
The front edge was always decorated with precious stones,
and the lappets at the sides were profusely embroidered.
At first the veil at the back hung down over the hair, which
was loose ; but later, as we shall see, the veil was split and
folded back over one side of the head-dress. In the latter
instances the hair seems to have been piled up under the
head-dress behind, as few of these examples show us the long
hair hanging down at the back.

1510—1520

ENGLAND at this period was the sole manufacturer of woollen stuffs; therefore wool, frieze, rugge, broadcloth, kersey, and similar materials were worn extensively by all classes, although the poor frequently wove their own homespun. Only the wealthy could afford such sumptuous fabrics as cloth of gold or silver, velvet, satin, tissue, tinsel, and fine damask, which were all imported at fabulous prices from France, Spain, and Italy. About 1515 a definite German tendency prevailed in England : heavy pleating and excessive slashing are noticeable on most garments, jerkins being so closely pleated as to consist almost entirely of three layers of material. Both the jerkin and gown assumed a yoke or collar similar at the back to a sailor-collar, and to this were attached the folded edges of the pleats, leaving the fold itself free and standing out from the garment instead of sewn flat as in the modern method of pleating. Such a gown is worn by the man on the left at the bottom of the page opposite. Sleeves became more and more excessive, longer and looser. Some were cut at the elbow or shoulder to allow them to hang loose, or to be tucked into the belt or girdle at the side and display the sleeve of the doublet or jerkin worn underneath.

Striped tights or hose, still worn a great deal on the Continent, were also frequently seen in England, but the mode of stocks with legs made from different coloured materials was seldom adopted on this side of the Channel.

Men's hair was still worn long, though usually cut in the manner of a longish " bob " in preference to the shoulder-length curls seen at the opening of the century.

1510—1520 (*continued*)

Four hundred years ago there were no middle-classes as we know them today. One was either a peasant, " one of the people," or else one belonged to the nobility, which included wealthy landowners and merchants. The working people's clothes were of necessity far simpler in cut and material than those worn by their employers, and we may safely assume that for the first half of the century there was little or no change in the apparel of either men or women among the peasants.

The men wore simply a shirt and tights, the latter of cloth reaching from waist to toe, covered by a belted doublet of some rough woollen material that finished an inch or two above the knee and had long sleeves. Their boots or shoes were usually made of leather and covered the ankle. Sometimes a cloak or gown was worn for extra warmth, and the flat cap, with a brim, similar to those already described, was seen everywhere.

Peasant women wore simple woollen garments, their shifts frequently made of linsey-woolsey. The gown itself (seen in the upper drawing on p. 23) was cut with a tight bodice, sometimes laced in the front, fairly close-fitting sleeves, and a full, short skirt barely reaching to the ankles. A large apron of holland or some coarser fabric was always worn, and the belt or girdle served to carry any small article that the housewife might require from time to time. The *coif* or cap was worn throughout the period, with modifications. Women's hose were of cloth and reached just above the knee, where they were tied ; shoes were of the loose slipper variety with a flat sole and round toes, and occasionally wooden shoes were worn in muddy localities.

About 1518 the " split " sleeve came into vogue for ladies of fashion. As may be seen in the costume illustrated here, the sides are caught together with gold clasps instead of the more usual " points." This mode remained in favour practically throughout the century.

1 5 1 0—1 5 2 0 (*continued*)

While a number of varied examples of women's apparel naturally appear in these pages, it should be understood that the nun-like head-dress and gown were still the most generally worn. The lady in black on the opposite page is, perhaps, the most typical Englishwoman. The rather exaggerated figure at the top right-hand corner is more representative of the Flemish or German style often seen in England at this time. The extravagant modes of slashing and tying with " points " were general in most European countries.

The unfortunate children of the sixteenth century were dressed as exact replicas of their parents, but this does not seem to have hindered them from playing such games as hoops, leap-frog, stool ball, and many others equally active. Babies were all swaddled or swathed until they reached the age of six months or more, the idea being that the legs and arms must necessarily grow straight if tied in that position. There is small wonder that infant mortality was so excessive ; the heat inside these swathings must have been unbearable during the summer months, and should the mother or nurse bind them too tight, the miserable child was doomed to deformity of the shoulders and thorax.

1 5 1 0—1 5 2 0 (*continued*)

The woman on the right at the bottom of the preceding page is wearing the gable head-dress with its lappets folded back to show the long side-pieces of the coif worn underneath. Hairdressing with this form of head-dress now assumes a mode of its own : either the hair was parted in the centre and the front part bound with ribbon and recrossed on the forehead, or—perhaps when the hair was thin or short—the front hair was encased in rolls of striped silk or cotton and arranged in a similar manner. The hair at the back was worn loose under the veil. Occasionally we find examples of the striped pad pushed farther back on the head and showing the centre parting of the hair in front, as may be seen among the group of heads on page 31.

The large velvet hats, slashed and decorated with gems and feathers, were not of English origin, but were brought over from Germany, France, and Spain. Several leading English ladies of the Court favoured these more masculine fashions. Anne Boleyn was rarely painted in anything nun-like, but her known portraits represent quite a valuable collection of rather masculine hats. The coif and the circlet of gold and gems with a short veil behind appeared about 1503, and seem to have remained in favour until supplanted by the Tudor cap made so popular by Mary Queen of Scots.

1520—1530

A NOTICEABLE change in the cut of the under-garment occurred about the 'twenties of this century. The neck-line gradually rose until it took the form of a minute frill—the first small beginning of the ruff to come. This fashion was more general for the man, women still preferring an open neck in most cases, although there are many examples of the high-necked shift.

Heavily embroidered materials gained brilliance by the addition of sewn pearls and beads and other semi-precious and precious stones. In the frontispiece is shown the first example of the treble sleeve, a fashion rigidly adhered to whenever the bell-shaped sleeve to the gown was worn. This consisted of a detachable short sleeve or cuff of a stiff embroidered material—in its early stages frequently striped ; worn over the lawn or cambric under-garment, and joined by "points," thus showing the under-sleeve, which was pulled out in puffs. This large cuff finished a few inches above the elbow, and, as the fashion progressed, became larger, until it formed a complete half-circle of stiff material folded and fastened in the manner described.

About 1525 the woman's skirt, which previously had been a complete affair, was cut up the front to form an inverted V, which disclosed a sumptuous embroidered petticoat, usually of contrasting colours to the gown or kirtle. A tendency to stiffen the petticoats and make the skirt stand away from the body was first noticeable about this date. The train also had practically disappeared from general use by about 1520, although it was still worn by ladies of the Court and for all ceremonious occasions; the train of this period was not the separate hanging train as we know it to-day, but the trailing point which was a feature of all gowns worn during the first twenty years of the sixteenth century.

The figure on the left at the bottom of the opposite page is an exceedingly interesting example of German fashions, a striking contrast to the very English lady facing her. There are few remaining examples of such pleated skirts, probably the weight of them was too much for the majority of women to bear, and the mode could not have existed for more than a very few years. It is, however amusing to note the amazing similarity between this figure and those of fashion plates of 1825-30. Fashions are forever changing—but never advancing.

1520—1530 (*continued*)

Of trunk-hose, the breeches are called " upper-stocks,"
and " nether-stocks " is the name for the stocking-like part
covering the foot, calf, and frequently the thigh. Practically
throughout the century these were joined together to form
one complete garment. The second man on the previous
page is wearing one of the earliest pairs of " paned " upper-
stocks, an effect achieved by slashing in even strips, or more
rarely by means of separate ribbon-like attachments of
embroidery. It will be noticed that as the century advanced
they became looser and were stuffed out to their fullest
capacity. This same man is also ornamented with
picadils, the folded and cut material visible on the shoulders,
wrists, and where the upper and nether stocks are
joined. This exceedingly popular form of decoration
was used by both sexes, and several examples, especially
as a shoulder and neck decoration, will be found in the
ensuing pages.

Shoes, which previously had been somewhat round-toed,
developed into the well-known square, padded, and slashed
shape in which Henry VIII was wont to be depicted. Sometimes these were ridiculously exaggerated, even to eight or
nine inches width at the toe, with tufts of coloured lining
pulled out through the slashes. They were tied at the ankle
with a thin leather lace, which came from behind the
heel of the shoe, not from the instep. On the page facing
is an example of loose *panes* tied just above the knee
to form yet a second bulge. At this early period, however, little or no stuffing was worn, merely a loose lining
which could be drawn out through the panes if the wearer
so desired.

1520—1530 (*continued*)

With the rise of the neck of the doublet and jerkin a small collar sometimes appeared, though this fashion seems to have been more military than civil until about 1535, when it became general.

The head-dresses illustrated here need little or no explanation. The gable at the bottom has the lappets folded and the veil split and laid back over the head-dress. The man next to this is wearing an exaggerated form of the traditional cap, and the loose, open pleats on his gown are clearly seen. The top left-hand figure is taken from a portrait of Anne Boleyn, and the gewgaw that hangs from the ridiculous cap is a typical addition.

It is impossible to over-emphasize the general extravagance of ornament among the wealthy. The amazing richness of embroidery, and the dazzling addition of jewels, could not conceivably be illustrated in a much larger book than this. If it be borne in mind that practically every square inch of the garments reproduced in these pages was ornamented, slashed, embroidered, and bejewelled, that magnificent pearls, jewels, and precious stones adorned practically every finger, trimmed every head-dress, decorated every neck, and were woven into every garment, then it may be possible to gain some idea of the extravagant splendour of a Court in the reign of Henry VIII. At no later period in the history of our country has the Court wallowed in so much gold and silver and priceless materials. And probably at no time have the poor been so squalidly housed and filthily garbed as they were during this amazing reign.

1530—1540

THE female example on the facing page is not, strictly speaking, the most typical of the period 1530-1540. It is, indeed, the German type of gown and hat adopted in England during the 'thirties, and rarely seen later than 1534. However, I have chosen it in this instance to give the reader some idea of the detail in design which I have already mentioned. Spot patterns and interchange designs were very popular, and the acanthus leaf figured extensively in all floral designs. The lady's gown or kirtle is of purple velvet, richly worked with silver thread; the lower part of the sleeve is white cloth-of-tissue with a traced design in gold. Under this she wears a pleated petticoat of yellow damask. The neck of the gown is heavily set with stones, and her belt and necklet are both of gold, with rubies and pearls inset. Her hat is of black velvet, also bravely adorned with many precious stones.

The gentleman beside her is a typical example of the fashionable Englishman of the late 'thirties. From now on a new item of men's clothing takes shape in the form of a waistcoat. The doublet is cut low to reveal the splendour of this beautifully embroidered and pearled garment. The latter in its turn is slashed to show off the fine lawn or satin shirt beneath. In this example the sleeves are made of the same material and design as the waistcoat, the doublet being sleeveless. The doublet is made of black velvet and decorated with bands of crewel-work, as is the skirt or base, which is split in front, showing the cod-piece, a feature of men's apparel until the 'eighties. The stocks are made of velvet, black at the top, and blue nether-stocks. Over all is the jerkin of light blue broadcloth lined with miniver; the elbow-length sleeves are slashed and show the fur linings.

1530—1540 (continued)

Let us for a moment imagine ourselves transported in time over four hundred years back to the scenes of Anne Boleyn's coronation. From the Tower to the Temple the city is alive with excitement. Cheapside, Cornhill, and Grace Street are marvellously decorated with gold and silver cloth and rich velvet hangings. The constables of the City, richly clad in velvet and silk, hold great staves in their hands to keep back the seething crowd of would-be spectators. From every gaily-trapped window excited and curious heads crane to get a glimpse of the new Queen.

Amid yells of applause and welcoming cheers the procession winds its way through the narrow, overcrowded streets. Foremost rides the Lord Mayor, splendid in his crimson velvet gown lined and trimmed with fur, his large gold chain flashing impressively in the sunlight. He is followed by footmen in white and red damask, then by twelve mounted Frenchmen clothed in blue velvet with blue and yellow sleeves, their horses' trappings a blue sarsenet ground with white crosses. Then proceeds a stately assortment of Knights, Squires, Judges, Gentlemen, Abbots, Barons, Bishops, Earls, and Marquises, these all gowned in scarlet or crimson. The Knights Commanders of the Bath wear gorgeous violet velvet, with hoods embroidered in gold and silver and " purled " with miniver !

Then at last, as we grow dizzy with so brilliant a spectacle, the Queen appears, a striking figure in white amongst such a riot of colour. Her litter of white cloth of gold is borne by two palfries in white damask. Her kirtle is of white cloth of tissue, her mantle of the same, wonderfully furred with ermine ; down her back hangs her fair hair, and on her head is a coif with a circlet about it full of rich and rare stones. And carried by four knights is the canopy of cloth of gold with gilt staves to shield her from the sun.

1530—1540 (continued)

Behind the Queen ride the Lord Chancellor and the Masters of the Horse; then come the ladies of the Court, all in scarlet velvet turned up with gold and tissue, their horses in magnificent trappings of cloth-of-gold. And, last of all, the gentlewomen of the Court are drawn in chariots of cloth-of-gold and clothed in scarlet and crimson. The procession passes, and a motley collection of shopkeepers, marketers, children, beggars, and sightseers crowd across the road, cheering. Such is the indelible picture that is left us by a contemporary historian. There are a thousand and one equally interesting details, especially of the feast: the amazing dishes they ate, the incredible quantity of wines and ales consumed, how Anne sat at the head of an immense table—her ladies to the left, gentlemen to the right—and was served with twenty-six dishes to each course.

This page of drawings and the one preceding it give various examples of the gradually changing style; the high neck for the shirt was practically always worn, and was finished with a *partlet strip*, or upstanding separate collar, which perhaps was the first version of the starched atrocity worn by men of to-day. A tiny shoulder-cape of velvet or cloth was often worn by ladies at this time, and a high-necked yoke of some material contrasting in colour with the gown seems to have been very popular until the 'fifties. Skirts were gradually becoming fuller and fuller, the hems just touching the ground all round.

1530—1540 (*continued*)

Several different types of caps were worn indoors by matrons and by domestics, and many varieties of the coif developed eventually into the upstanding semicircular head-dress, of which the top right-hand illustration is an example. This was so heavy with jewels and ornaments that it had to be tied under the chin with a narrow white cord to stop it sliding down the back of the wearer's head.

From about 1535 men's caps began to be worn with the brim down, instead of turned up as had previously been the case. The same style of cap was adopted by many ladies and worn over the coif. Between the years 1530 and 1540 a short bowl-like cut of the hair was introduced for men— a transition stage between the " bob " and the short hair fashionable for half a century from about 1545 ; an instance of this style appears on the next page, worn by the boy in blue. Ear-pieces, cut to cover the ears and nape of the neck, were apparently quite a regular addition to many caps, both for men and women. Sometimes a close velvet cap with ear-flaps and a cord under the chin was worn, this seems to have been called a " night cap," though whether it was worn day and night is impossible to say.

1540—1550

HERE is an example of the bell-skirt without folds, cut across the weave of the material to give the skirt the flared effect at the hem. In its earliest stages it is doubtful whether any actual wire structure was worn ; the full, creaseless effect was probably obtained by padding at the hip and by a stiffened hem, combined with the addition of numerous petticoats. However, with the introduction of the Spanish *vertingale* about fifteen or twenty years later, there appears little or no difference in the outline except, perhaps, for an added width of hem.

There was a general tendency to tightness of contour about 1540. The sleeves, for instance, previously soft and malleable, became stiff and somewhat bulky, owing to a certain extent to the increased embroidery on the surface of the materials, and also to the craze for bombasting or stiffening which was just beginning to be noticeable. High leather corsets were generally worn by ladies of fashion, and these were responsible for the curious bolster-like effect so evident in Holbein's portraits.

A dress with a yoke nearly always seems to have had a high stand-up collar open in front. There are also a few examples of the yoked dress finishing with a minute ruff. In the example opposite the yoke is made of fur, but instances of this are rare.

The bonnet-like cap worn by the small boy is certainly amusing and not wholly devoid of charm ; it was apparently worn solely by children and elderly men. The other child has his jerkin guarded with the fashionable narrow black bands.

1540—1550 (*continued*)

It is exceedingly difficult to find contemporary examples of the costume of serving men and women of this period— no doubt few, if any, ever had the opportunity of sitting for their portraits. An excellent example, however, is reproduced in each of the drawings opposite. The woman's dress is particularly interesting, and shows us that pleated petticoats were in general use ; the little striped cap is of an unusual shape, in fact I have been unable to find more than three or four similar examples, and one of these was made of fur. The idea of fastening the skirt to the belt was probably to protect it from getting unnecessarily spotted in front, for although the effect obtained is in itself exceedingly becoming, it is doubtful whether such was the chief consideration.

Two interesting points to note in the male figure at the top are, firstly, the *mock coat*, a cloak with sleeves entirely for ornamentation ; and, secondly, the upper stocks or breeches which, as is typical in these garments' early stages, have a tight-fitting hip-yoke, the *panes* only beginning from the top of the leg, and reaching half-way down the thigh. In this instance they are joined slantwise. The huge square shoulders, padded and bombasted, reached their height of absurdity during this decade, and slowly sank back to a more normal form. At the close of Henry VIII's reign (he died in 1547) shoes began to be made with leather or velvet, covering the instep, and with an inch or so of added protection for the heel. The toes, still squarish, were less exaggerated, and slashing was made in some instances both sideways and upwards. With the death of the King fashions seemed suddenly to mark time, and until the accession of Elizabeth in 1558 very little change took place.

1540—1550 (*continued*)

Bodices or stomachers of gowns gradually assumed a point in front, in preference to the straight line at the waist. About 1545, and for some five years later, they were fastened down the front, the opening being faced with jewels or embroidery and stiffened with wooden busks.

Little girls were forcibly corsetted at a ridiculously early age, and quite probably this was the cause of the deformed shoulders of so many women mentioned by contemporary historians, both at this date and later in the century. It certainly seems impossible, to our modern minds, that any child's bones could develop in a normal manner when hampered with corsets which not only reached from armpits to hips, but were made of leather, wood, or even metal. But these ancestors of ours must have been amazingly hardy. They lived and died surrounded by such an odd mixture of revolting cruelty, dirt, and disease on the one hand, and on the other sumptuous wealth, splendour, and bravery seemingly out of all perspective. Their streets were so foul with drainage and rubbish that clogs, or *chopins*, had to be worn to lift their feet above the filth. Yet their damp and draughty halls were decorated with priceless tapestries, furnished with wonderful hand-carved furniture, and hung with beautiful damasks ; their tables were set with gold and silver cups and platters, and their kitchens richly and plentifully supplied with every conceivable variety of meat, fish, and fowl.

1540—1550 (continued)

These sixteenth-century Englishmen were compounded of paradox. They could apparently witness, merely as interested spectators, an acquaintance being hanged, drawn, and quartered. They could set out in small ships to discover new worlds and face unknown dangers. And yet they were terrified of witchcraft, and wore charms and amulets to avert the evil eye, and consulted oracles, and indulged in love-potions in all seriousness. They grumbled and worried over the problem of traffic-control in the City, and over the price of meat when it rose from three-farthings a pound to one penny. At times they were so strangely like ourselves, and at times such worlds apart. Their persons reflected these extremes, especially in the lack of fastidiousness beneath gorgeous exteriors. Baths were considered unnecessary and unhealthy, fresh air was bad for the lungs, sweet scents were held by most to be evil—cloying the senses and there-fore inviting the devil. Small wonder that when Henry walked abroad he carried in his hand " an Orange whereof the substance had been taken out and filled up with a sponge full of vinegar and other confections against the Pestilent Ayres, the which he most commonly held to his nose in a press."

Men's caps became gradually larger in the crown until crown and brim were almost the same width ; the crown was higher, too, than formerly, and somewhat stiffer. About 1550, ruffles came into being. At first, however, they were devoid of starch, which was not discovered until some ten years later ; they were made of holland or lawn and, as will be seen in the illustration, somewhat irregular in form. The tiny ruffle at the top of the *partlet* strip was quite general for both sexes.

1550—1560

DURING this decade the people of England were under three successive sovereigns, each totally different in character and qualities, and their changing influences reacted noticeably upon the style and cut of clothes, even if there was no great variety in costume until after Mary's death.

The first three years, under the youthful Edward VI, saw little or no change. The boy was delicate, and the country seemed to stand still, waiting to see what would happen next. But with the accession of Mary, and the introduction of a Spanish prince as king, fashions began to change. Various Spanish styles were brought into the country, the chief of them the *vertingale*, or farthingale, a somewhat similar affair to the crinoline of the nineteenth century. An amazing variety of new head-dresses and caps supplanted the rather hackneyed coif-and-circlet and the gable head-dress, and for men a hat took the place of the flat cap in many instances. Throughout her reign Mary herself clung tenaciously to the old styles, and innovations were certainly not adopted with any display of interest on her part ; the Court, therefore, was practically compelled to adhere to the high-waisted, bell-sleeved gowns, and the coif or caul with the circlet. The caul head-dress with the circlet disappeared at the end of Mary's reign, and probably it was cast aside with a sigh of relief. Most certainly it was exceedingly awkward and heavy to carry, and we read of Mary's coronation that " she wore . . . on her head a caule of cloth of tinsel beset with pearl and stone, and above the same a round circlet of gold beset so richly with precious stones that the value thereof was infinite. The same caule and circlet being so massive and ponderous that she was fayne to bear up her head with her hand." She must have had a ghastly headache after the twelve-hour ceremony.

1550—1560 (*continued*)

In the year 1556 the Ambassador of the Emperor of Russia came to England to pay his respects to Mary and Philip, and there is an interesting list of the gifts showered upon him to take back to the Emperor, which reflects the amazing value set on fine raiment :

" First, two rich pieces of cloth of tissue.
Item, one fine piece of scarlet.
Item, one fine violet in graine.
Item, one azure cloth.
Item, a notable paire of brigandine, with a murian covered with crimson velvet, and gilt nails."

A personal gift to the Ambassador from the Queen included :

" One rich piece of cloth of tissue, a piece of cloth of gold, another piece of cloth of golde raised with crimson velvet, a piece of crimson velvet in graine, a piece of damask purpled, a piece of purple velvet and a piece of crimson damask."

So overjoyed with this wonderful gift was the Emperor that he promptly returned the compliment by having large quantities of rare furs and live animals shipped to the Queen of England. History unfortunately does not state whether these fine beasts were immediately slaughtered for their magnificent fur, or if they were kept as royal pets.

The five years of Mary's reign were among the cruellest and most cold-blooded in our history, yet we find details of these polite international exchanges of pieces of cloth described at far greater length than any of the epoch-making slaughters or executions, possibly because the latter were too numerous and commonplace to be commented upon.

1 5 5 0—1 5 6 0 (*continued*)

The bell-shaped sleeve totally disappeared with the accession of Elizabeth in 1558. The new style favoured a tight-fitting sleeve with a large "puff" at the shoulder and a tiny frill or ruffle at the wrist. This puff was frequently quite separate, or it might belong to the gown and the sleeve itself be separate. The new arrangement was equally popular for men's wear. The full bombasted and slashed sleeves never quite lost favour throughout this reign; about the year 1590, indeed, they became even more popular than at any previous date.

Mantles, or *surcotes*, with short puff sleeves were worn, even indoors at times, their fullness increasing at the hem to give an idea of even folds from top to bottom. Many examples of these delightfully formal garments may be seen upon the effigies on contemporary tombs; but in such instances it is quite impossible, owing to the absurd effect of any but the simplest drapery on a recumbent figure, to obtain any idea of the Spanish *vertingale* or full-bottomed skirt which was undoubtedly worn at that time.

Probably the reason for so many changes in fashion about 1558–1600 was that Elizabeth was a comparatively bright young person, who had been imprisoned and suppressed for many years. The effect of sudden access to practically unlimited wealth and freedom and power was that she promptly stocked her wardrobe with all the gowns she desired. We certainly know that she was fond of clothes— at one time in her life at least she possessed three thousand dresses at once, or so historians tell us. In fact, Richmond Palace was called the Queen's wardrobe, being practically filled with her gowns that were not in use.

1550—1560 (*continued*)

With the introduction of new styles of head-dress the centre parting became less general. The hair was brushed back from the forehead rather loosely to make a slight puff round the face, and later was padded on either side so that it might fill the curve of the cap, as may be seen on the page facing. The heart-shaped cap, commonly associated with Mary Queen of Scots, became amazingly fashionable and continued in fashion with many slight alterations until caps ceased to be worn. They were at first worn over a small embroidered cap, as seen at the top of the previous page.

Heavily embroidered and jewelled bands of material seem to have been the most popular method of decoration for most garments, and of course *picadils* were still as popular. Bone-lace was also used a great deal, both as a trimming and as a hat-band for men. Heavy gold neck-chains were not as popular as the narrow cord or ribbon, with a locket attached ; the locket either carried a portrait of a lover, some precious stone, or a tiny miniature. Women wore similar cords tied round their waists, and on these a rosary was sometimes worn. Ear-rings were very popular for both sexes, the gallant often preferring to wear only one. Small ruffles were worn by practically everyone, for the huge turn-down collar became more popular in the 'sixties.

1560—1570

SOME account of the development of trunk-hose has already been given, but this example conveys a better idea of their actual structure than any written explanation. In surviving contemporary specimens it is not until those of the 'sixties that we can see with any clearness how these trunk-hose were composed; but when the jerkin no longer covers the doublet several excellent examples are forthcoming. Although the *panes* are clearly shown in the costume illustrated here, it should be explained that the "drawings-out" were in most cases definitely fuller than these. Sometimes as many as a dozen yards of material were used in the stuffing of one pair, and if this was particularly fine it was pulled out several inches beyond the *panes*.

From about 1565 breeches began to assume gigantic proportions, and, although the cut seems to have varied, the common practice was to stuff them with bran, wool, hair, rags, or anything else that might be at hand. Soldiers found them particularly useful for storing loot. So absurdly large did they become that a scaffold was erected in the Houses of Parliament "for those to sit on who used the wearing of great breeches stuffed with hair like wool sacks." Apparently it was impossible to sit with any degree of comfort on an ordinary chair. What method was adopted in the home to make seating possible it is difficult to say; there are no records of chairs differing in structure, in fact existing examples of Elizabethan furniture show us that few chairs were without arms.

1560—1570 (*continued*)

In the year 1564 starch was introduced into England by a certain Mistress Dingham Vander Plasse. So great was the demand for education in starching that she started a school of instruction in the composition of starch, and charged several pounds for imparting this knowledge to young ladies of rank. The problem of laundering was solved, and ruffles began to grow enormously in size. But this knowledge took several years to filter down through the masses, and not until the 'seventies was the large " ruff " worn by everyone. There are several existing prints representing the laundering and forming of ruffs during the 'seventies and 'eighties of the sixteenth century.

Starch in its earliest days was tinted yellow, so that the first big ruffles were invariably creamy in colour. The fashion died, however, when a certain notorious Mrs. Turner was hanged at Tyburn in one of these yellow ruffles. After this gruesome episode the modish shade turned from yellow to blue, probably very little different in its palest tints from the starch we use to-day. Frequently the ruff was untied in front to give a little more air and freedom to the wearer, for it is difficult to imagine any form of neck-wear more uncomfortable than a closed ruff. Large upstanding collars were worn by women who did not favour the ruffle, and the turned-down collar already mentioned was worn by men. The neck was not visible again until the 'nineties of the century, but there are numerous instances of a gown itself finishing with a low, square line at the shoulders so that a considerable expanse of bare chest was visible under the ruffle and above the gown.

1560—1570 (*continued*)

During the year 1565 the problem of unemployment in cloth-manufacturing towns became chronic, because so many imported silks and velvets were used that there was little or no demand for the woollens and cottons manufactured in England. An appeal was made to the Queen, who issued a proclamation forbidding any further importation of materials from the Continent, and further ordering that every man should wear a woollen cap unless he had an income of over forty pounds a year. Whether these official commands made any impression on the people is difficult to say, but it is certain that the effect, if any, was not lasting, because garments, instead of losing brilliance, seem to have become even more rich and ornate than before. And the woollen cap was not nearly as popular as the velvet one, or as the more fashionable hat. If the Queen had followed up her proclamation by herself appearing in some woollen or cotton gown instead of the exaggerated foreign styles she invariably adopted, the royal decrees might have been more effective.

The first figure on the opposite page is wearing an excellent example of the Spanish *vertingale* or farthingale, and the general use of small slashes and picadils is shown. It is difficult to exaggerate the importance attached to details at this period : the garments illustrated here may appear comparatively simple, but in reality they were crowded with minute designs, lace, embroidery, guards and gold *aglets* (small eyelet holes for the " points ").

At the bottom of the opposite page the female figure with pleated skirt, on the left, is wearing the traditional costume, worn in many of the German States. It was not an English fashion, but we may safely assume that similar costumes, worn by visitors or foreign domestics, were frequently seen in this country.

1560—1570 (*continued*)

A little may be said here about the wearing of beards in the Sixteenth Century. For the first twenty years of the period men were clean-shaven. Henry VIII, however, started to grow a beard at about the age of twenty-three, and a few years afterwards the mode became popular among the nobility. By 1545 the fashion had spread, and beards were far more prevalent than clean-shaven faces. The pointed beard and small pointed moustache first came into vogue during the 'fifties, probably another introduction from Spain by Philip. The beard became gradually smaller and neater until the 'nineties, and by about 1600 had assumed the size and shape of a small triangular postage-stamp stuck in the middle of the chin. Tiny moustaches with no beard were also fashionable from about 1570 to the end of the century.

The two upper head-dresses on opposite page are interesting in that they represent some of the amusing transitional stages between head-dresses and hats, the one on the right being distinctly reminiscent of the policeman's helmet of to-day. Men's hats with a large brim and a shallow crown were not worn for more than a few years in this decade ; they were followed by a craze for high crowns, but became popular again during the late 'eighties. Caps at this time had little or no brim, but a band of lace, embroidery, or jewels was usually worn as a form of decoration.

1570—1580

WITH the 'seventies came several entirely new fashions for men. The doublet began to develop a sort of padded and stiffened point in front, whence it was commonly known as the " peascod-belly " doublet, of which one of the earliest examples is illustrated here ; this fashion became ridiculously exaggerated during the 'eighties. The *mandilion* was almost as popular as the cloak ; it was a short, full coat or jerkin with hanging sleeves, the sides often split to show the doublet underneath. Cloaks were most fashionable, short, barely reaching to the hips, and sometimes worn swathed round in the Venetian style, as may be seen on the left-hand figure at the foot of the next page. Shoulder-padding was general, and " wings " were added to accentuate the width of the doublet.

Short stockings called boot-hose were worn under the boot to save the hose from unnecessary friction ; similar in shape to the golf-stocking of to-day, they were made of rich materials and beautifully embroidered. Venetians, a species of knee-breeches, bombasted, quilted, and padded, came into vogue about 1572. These usually reached just to the knee, and were either tied with a wide garter or finished with a small frill or band. Whenever trunk-hose were worn they were so abbreviated as barely to cover the buttocks, and as the peascod doublet became more exaggerated the trunks developed into a mere small roll a few inches deep, sometimes hardly visible under the huge doublet in front. It should be remembered here that after about 1550 the term " upper-stocks " was dropped in favour of the more general " trunk-hose," so that in describing hose the roll or pumpkin-like top was usually called " trunk-hose," and the leg covering itself termed " nether-stocks."

1 5 70—1 5 80 *(continued)*

About six or seven years after the introduction of " Venetians," yet another new style came into being—trunk-hose
with canions. A loose stocking-like appendage was attached
to the padded trunks and reached just below the knee ; the
nether-stocks were separate and drew up like a stocking over
the canions, fastening with a garter either just above or
below the knee. One of the earliest examples of this style
is to be seen on the lower left-hand figure on the
opposite page. An interesting variation of the trunk-hose,
especially amusing for its plus-fours appearance, is worn
by the upper left-hand figure. This variation was, however, of German or Swiss origin, and not frequently seen
in England. When this style was worn the padding was
all of loose material, not bombast, and the drawings-out
through the panes were sometimes so liberal that the panes
themselves were practically invisible.

Silks, velvets, satins, damasks, sarcenet, taffeta, and châlet
were the most popular materials. Although all these were
imported, the old trouble of unemployment in manufacturing
towns seems by this time to have been to some degree
avoided by the large export trade in wools, kerseys, dozens,
penistone cottons, fustians, buffins, cameleons, linsey-woolsey,
and many other interesting materials. All these apparently
were not suitable foundations for the exquisite tailoring and
abundant embroidery lavished on practically all English
garments at this time.

About this time Elizabeth was presented with a pair of
silk stockings woven by one of her ladies, and after wearing
these she decided to dispense with any other form of hose.
Whether she was actually the first person in England to wear
hand-knitted stockings it is difficult to say—there are records
of Edward VII having a pair of silk hose given him, and
apparently they were hand-knitted. However, after the
'sixties silk nether-stocks became exceedingly fashionable in
spite of the fact that as much as five pounds was paid for a
single pair.

1 5 7 0—1 5 8 0 *(continued)*

Women's clothes also became more exaggerated in style. One particularly new garment was the transparent cobweb lawn cloak or veil, with a large, upstanding, heart-shaped collar, in some cases closely resembling a hood. These cloaks or veils often reached to the ground, and were decorated with a tiny edge of lace.

Towards the end of this decade came the French *vertingale* or farthingale. This was vastly different from the Spanish vertingale in that the contour, instead of being cone-shaped, was more like that of a drum with the upper rim tilted down in the front. This effect was obtained with the help of a large whalebone frame of cart-wheel shape fitted to the hips and tipped up at the back by shortening the spoke-like attachments. The skirt worn over this was exceedingly full, and shorter than any other form of dress at this period. Sometimes a similar effect was obtained by the wearing of a bolster-like padding tied round the waist. There were many variations of this fashion: sometimes a short, loosely gathered basque was worn over the skirt finishing at the hoop, and later an immense ruffle, similar to the ones worn about the neck, was attached to the waist and reached out to the edge of the drum. The Spanish farthingale did not lose its popularity with the introduction of the French, and in some contemporary paintings we can see clearly that the skirt was sometimes held out by means of a single hoop at the hem and a little padding at the waist.

1570—1580 (*continued*)

Hats now began to assume a jaunty and, to us, an amusing
aspect. Beaver—alluded to as a curious kind of hair—was
quite popular by about 1578. Sarcenet, wool, taffeta, and
velvet were all used in the making of hats. Ladies often
wore them over a tight-fitting cap. The hat-band was a
specially valuable possession, as this was frequently adorned
with precious stones and pearls.

Contemporary moralists wrote scathingly of the absurdities
of fashion, and particularly of the wickedness of using
cosmetics. One such writer took it upon himself to deliver
this awful warning: "Those which paint or colour themselves in this world otherwise than God hath made them,
let them feare lest when the daie of judgement commeth the
Lorde will not knowe them for his creatures."

Writers of this period seem to have been divided into two
definite classes: Those who indulged in every possible
extravagance and excuse for indecency in their literary efforts,
and stern moralists who, in their somewhat wild efforts to
crush extravagance, rigorously damned everything pertaining
to beauty, cleanliness, fastidiousness, or general improvements.
The former upheld the gaiety and brilliance of Court life, the
feasting, drinking, and general debauchery, and they give us
a fairly accurate account of the life of any young gallant
who was not afraid to sow sufficient wild-oats to drive him
out of his town, or even out of the country, for a few years.

1580—1590

THE peascod doublet reached the height, or depth, of absurdity during these ten years ; after about 1590 few exaggerated styles were to be seen. Not only were these doublets exceedingly hot and bulky for the unfortunate wearer, but he experienced great difficulty in any endeavour to stoop. So stuffed, bombasted, and quilted did they become that the points actually reached some eight or nine inches below the belt. The idea of the unitiated appears to have been that these doublets were designed especially to further " gourmandie and gluttonie." As eating and drinking was one of the chief pastimes during the latter part of the century, there may have been some truth in so sweeping an assertion, and consideration of the figures illustrated on the next page makes it easy to sympathize with this view. When we read of the amazing dishes of capons, larks, sparrows, roast oxen, boars' heads, and innumerable pies—including, of course, the then rare delicacy, " potato pyes "—that were habitually consumed at one sitting, it is hard to avoid believing that some sort of camouflage for undue stoutness was necessary.

The *Anatomie of Abuses* suggests that the exaggerated fashions worn at this time were not altogether approved, even by their wearers : " For moste of our new-fangled fashions dooe thei not rather deforme us than adorne us, disguise us than become us, makyng us rather semble savage Beastes and sterne monsters than continent sober christians ? " Probably this reasonable point of view accounts for the comparatively short popularity of the peascod belly in this country. Nevertheless it is the period immortalized by Punch and Judy, for even to-day Punch may be seen with his ruffle and peascod doublet.

1580—1590 (*continued*)

During the 'seventies and 'eighties, the traditional type of wear for scholars was a long coat, similar to that now worn by the boys at Christ's Hospital. At the bottom of the facing page an example of this can be seen in its original form with a ruffle. Beneath the coat, knee-breeches were worn, similar probably to those worn by the male figure on the right. This figure is wearing a hunting tunic, but his tight-fitting breeches are not in accordance with the prevailing fashions for general wear at that time.

Particularly interesting from the theatrical designer's point of view is the plaited stomacher and hat-band worn by the first female figure at the top of the page.

Until the end of the century the long overcoats, which hung from the shoulders to the ground in deep folds, were worn loose, or tied at the waist, when the bulk of the gown beneath was not too great to make a belt impracticable.

1580—1590 (*continued*)

Women started to frizz and crimp their hair during the 'eighties, and, as the " puffed " effect grew in favour, wire frames were devised to support their frizzed and curled locks. " Wreaths " and " borders " were arranged across the top of the head from ear to ear ; these were sometimes imitation flowers, or even precious stones set in a gold or silver framework. Wigs and added pieces of hair became popular, and dyes were used so extensively that a lady of fashion was rarely seen at two succeeding functions with her hair the same shade. As additional decorations, rings, beads, pearls, precious stones, and other gewgaws were fixed among the curls in a manner called enchanting by contemporaries. The hair apparently became a nesting-place for any extra piece of jewellery that could not be affixed elsewhere.

Elizabeth herself specialized in wigs, red and a sort of saffron colour being her two favourite shades. Some fashionable ladies not blessed with such an abundance of hair as their more fortunate sisters, and probably unwilling to go to the expense of buying wigs, bribed peasant women and children to part with their locks for a few pence, and thus added to their inadequate supply of crowning glory. The hair being eventually arranged or " laid out " to the wearer's satisfaction, a large velvet or beaver hat was perched on the front or side of the head ; these hats were similar to those worn by men and invariably had a feather worn in the hat-band.

1580—1590 (*continued*)

It will be noticed that whenever the French farthingale was worn a stiff V-shaped stomacher invariably accompanied it. This was worn at a slight angle to the body, fitting at the breast and gradually sloping outwards, till the base of the V rested on the tilted front of the farthingale. In several portraits of the time the hand is hidden behind this, which means that in some cases the stomacher must have been worn loose. Tight-lacing was exceedingly prevalent, and there are records that " since busks came in request horn is scarce." Girls endeavoured to make their waists so small that they could span them with their hands. This wasp-waist outline was augmented by the use, above and below the corset, of " little bolsters or pillows for to seem more fat and comely." The shoulders were padded and the sleeves bombasted in violent contrast to the small waist.

Ruffles during the 'eighties became so large and unwieldy that an under-prop was devised to lift them up. Sometimes the ruffle was pinned to the ears ; in other instances it fell down over the shoulders.

Cork-soled shoes called *pinsnets* and *pantoffles* were worn ; these had a heel about an inch or an inch and a half high, and their wearers had great difficulty in managing to walk with them. So uncomfortable were they that frequently men's legs swelled from wearing them. Every possible colour and material was used in the making of these shoes.

Hose made from jernsey, worsted, crewell, yarn, thread, and of course the most fashionable silk, were dyed as many different colours as the shoes. An interesting list of fashionable shades includes " russet, saffron, black, white, red, grene, yellowe, watchet, blew and pink." Scabbards and sheaths were made from velvet and even embroidered linen.

1580—1590 (*continued*)

Ladies at this time wore beautifully embroidered and scented gloves and shoes or " pumps " made of cheverill, silk, or velvet. When walking abroad they carried black velvet masks to shield their complexions from the sun, or to disguise them from undesirable acquaintances. Fans with silver handles were very popular, and practically every woman carried a small hand-mirror either attached to her girdle or hanging on a cord about her neck. These looking-glasses were rudely alluded to as " Devil's Spectacles " by contemporary moralists—" And good reason, else how could they see the devil in themselves ? "

Apparently rather childish and demure mannerisms, and a craze for " baby-talk," were adopted by the most fashionable ladies. These must have seemed more than a little absurd, and in violent contrast to their stiff, bombasted appearances— and, by all accounts, their ultra-sophisticated and immoral behaviour. Let it be said at once that at least Elizabeth did not set the vogue for " baby-talk " ; her vocabulary would probably shock even the broadest-minded of men of to-day. Shakespeare does not give the impression that a mincing of words was the general trend of the time, and his works are amazingly discreet compared with others written at the same period. Men were certainly somewhat coarse in their behaviour, even if effeminate in their apparel : spitting, tobacco - chewing, and tooth - picking were all reckoned elegant accomplishments.

1590—1600

THE century ends in a wild orgy of extravagance. Even the country people, previously content with their russet smocks and *mockados*, now emulated their superiors in every conceivable manner and blossomed out in silks and satins whenever in any way possible, selling their last cow or pig to buy a pair of fine silk hose to excite the envy of their less well-apparelled neighbours. Clothes seem to have become the principal consideration in life, and so many and varied were the styles for men that the fop or gallant could hardly have one suit completed before it was out of fashion. In Ben Jonson's *Everyman out of his Humour*, the young collegiate tries desperately to keep pace with the latest demands of fashion, and in consequence gets head-over-heels in debt, because as fast as his tailor turns out one style he sees another which is newer and therefore more desirable. The fashionable lady is seen vividly and entertainingly through the eyes of a contemporary poet :

> . . . Wear curled Periwigs and chalk their faces
> And still are gazing in their pocket glasses.
> Tyred with pinned ruffles, fans and partlet-strips
> With Buskes and Vertingales about their hips.
> And tread on Corked Stilts at pris'nor's pace,
> And make their napkin for their spitting place.

The whole century was such a comical mixture of polished indecency and crude exquisiteness that it is only after reading dozens of contemporary volumes that we can hope to obtain even a glimmering understanding of these ancestors of ours. Doubtless an Elizabethan gentleman landed suddenly amongst us to-day would consider our modes and manners equally inconsistent and amusing.

1590—1600 (*continued*)

The magnificent costume illustrated here provides an interesting example of sixteenth-century design.   Some time during the 'eighties a fashion for depicting scenes, animals, birds, fishes, or anything which might be a typical emblem of the wearer, had been adopted as a motif for design.   This particular petticoat—drawn from a garment belonging to Elizabeth—is probably intended to show some of the beasts, flowers, fish, and fowl to be found in her dominions, and the foreign waters explored by her sea captains.   There is also an existing portrait of Sir Francis Drake, in the National Portrait Gallery, apparently painted soon after his circumnavigation, which clearly shows small worlds, each encircled by a complete ring, embroidered on his doublet.

Ladies' stomachers or doublets were often cut from the same pattern as men's, and even at this early date we find the now time-worn assertion that women were aping men, and trying to appear masculine to the detriment of their natural charms.   Though how a richly embroidered doublet with a lace-edged ruffle, worn over exaggeratedly full skirts, could be termed masculine it is difficult to comprehend.

Men's hair was worn frequently shoulder-length, and about 1595 a fashion for " ear-locks "—later termed lovelocks—became very popular with young men.   The hair in this case was allowed to grow in front so that it hung down in two locks, one either side of the face, and rested in a curl on each shoulder ; the back, however, was kept short.

Practically any shape or size of hat might be fashionable during the 'nineties.   High-crowned and small-brimmed, or low-crowned and large-brimmed, were each equally smart if worn with a cable hat-band.   Some crowns were so high that they rose twelve or fifteen inches above the head.   All colours and practically any material might be used in the making up of these hats.

1590—1600 (*continued*)

Trunk-hose with canions assumed two definite formations. One, the unbroken roll round the hips, as seen on several earlier pages, and the other somewhat square in effect, slightly resembling a miniature farthingale ; three of these will be seen on the previous page. *Panes* either developed into a formal series of embroidered bands, with nothing of the padding or lining visible, or else became sufficiently small and narrow for the drawings-out to be evenly arranged to cover them. The latter arrangement gave the appearance of an equally-gathered piece of material, as is shown in the last coloured plate.

The skirt of the doublet at this time was cut up to form overlapping tabs similar in appearance to the "tassets" worn on armour. One other form of breeches that became a "rage" during the last decade of the century were the "open-breeches." These were perfectly straight, un-gathered trousers, that reached a few inches below the knees, similar in cut to a rather elongated pair of modern shorts, or an abbreviated pair of trousers. Usually these were embroidered, and a tendency to decorate the hem with coloured ribbon or bone-lace ultimately developed into the lace-edged, flapping nether-garments of the Cavalier of the Stuart period.

1590—1600 *(continued)*

So we draw to the close of the most interesting century in our history, a century shaken by the discovery of a New World, yielding untold wealth for any man to exploit. The people, in their crazed enthusiasm over the New World, burst into wild orgies of expenditure. Illimitable adventure awaited them across the seas. Why should they be afraid of adventure in their own country ? If a fortune were gambled away in one single night, what matter ? Could not they sail forth, as others had done, to an unknown El Dorado, and come back in galleons laden with all manner of precious stones and great bars of gold and silver ? No sober-minded stay-at-homes were they. And the spirit of adventure, bravery, and extravagance must needs be given expression— hence the dazzling array of costumes, the exotic materials, and the priceless decorations set forth in these pages.